Margaret Ryan

Songs of Rememberance

Margaret Ryan

Songs of Rememberance

ISBN/EAN: 9783337007027

Printed in Europe, USA, Canada, Australia, Japan

Cover: Foto ©Thomas Meinert / pixelio.de

More available books at **www.hansebooks.com**

SONGS

OF

REMEMBRANCE

BY

MARGARET RYAN

("Alice Esmonde.")

DUBLIN
M. H. GILL AND SON
O'CONNELL STREET
1889

TO

MY BROTHER'S MEMORY

IN SORROWFUL LOVE AND REVERENCE,

I INSCRIBE THIS BOOK.

M. R.

These Poems appeared in *The Irish Monthly* at intervals, from the second yearly volume to the present—at first with the writer's initials appended, and then, as these were the same as the Editor's, under the name of "Alice Esmonde."

CONTENTS.

SONGS OF REMEMBRANCE.

BEREAVEN.

Keep strong, O heart, keep strong and brave,
  Keep true unto thy inmost core,
As true as to the moon yon wave,
  Whose foam rims white the wreck-strewn shore.

Keep strong as love, keep true as death,
  That tracks love's steps through patient years,
Keep faithful till thy latest breath
  To one fond trust held fresh in tears.

Make in thy life a sacred place,
  A room closed fast without a stair ;
And see thou let no strange cold face
  Gaze idly on thy pictures there.

2

But shouldst thou meet some aching heart,
   Grown pitiful from hours of pain,
Grown kind from sorrow's chastening smart,
   Let such in reverence weep again.

Hang low thy pictures round each wall,
   The frames once gold-edged black and deep,
Where death's chill hand swept over all,
   And grave-dews on the canvas weep.

See, some are drawn where home-light lies—
   That light extinguished in such woe—
And more are scenes from southern skies
   Where cactus bloom, and citrons grow.

'Twere sweet to wander there once more,
   A pilgrim tear-stained and unknown;
For one to stand, where two before
   Had stood—alone, ah me! alone.

See, some are black with woe and fear;
   Death's awful shadow hovering nigh:
O Christ, my God, in pity hear!
   I kissed his brow and did not die.

O hopes more sickening than despair!
   O long, dark night of death and pain!
O swift, wild cries of urgent prayer!
   You shiver through my soul again.

Who'd sing life's songs of saddest note ?
   Who'd build on joys that change and die ?
Is death not death's sole antidote ?
   And does not death o'er all rule high ?

Does not the best fall in its prime,
   And things the fairest fold decay ?
Will peace not come in God's good time ?
   Who would prolong this darkened day ?

We've walked our last in summer fields,
   Poor heart ! we wait not other springs,
We grasp but fruit that sorrow yields—
   A blight has fallen on dearer things.

Our sun has set, our blossoms dead,
   Our roses withered one and all,
Our birds to brighter bowers have fled :
   All things we loved gone past recall.

And when you fail, sad heart, and lie,
   Unwept, uncared for, and unknown,
And when you break, poor heart ! and die,
   With none but God to hear your moan :

None but the Lord who pitieth much,
   He that bled sore and suffered too,
None but His Mother's hand to touch
   Where you were wounded through and through.

We look for some such hour as this :
   The path is rough and dim the way,
We drank of rapture and of bliss ;
   We wait to die alone some day.

And then we'll drink of bliss again,
   Of rapture deeper, more complete,
Within that Land where never pain
   Nor parting comes when friends once meet.

These golden gates will open wide,
   We shall pass in and never leave.
Oh, think, poor heart, so sorely tried,
   The day comes fast no more to grieve.

In Memory of October 29th, 1885.

A MOUNTAIN ROSE.

I KNOW a rose upon a mountain far,
   A white and crimson flower that never dies,
That sends its perfume to the farthest star,
      Clear past the moon and skies.

It has a web of brier wove close around,
   'Tis fenced about with thorns that pierce and
     smart,
And very freely on the prickly ground
      My feet bleed—and my heart.

I leave the glad vales smiling every morn,
   The sweet home sunshine on the fields behind,
I leave the reapers singing 'mid the corn
      That wiser hands will bind;

I walk a lonesome road.   I hush all strife ;
   Sometimes the air is very cold and fine ;
Sometimes I'd give my heart's blood and my life,
      If that one flower was mine.

'Tis hard to bear the wind, the rain, and sleet :
   To shiver in the cold where dead leaves fall ;
But rest will be the sweeter—and more sweet
      One day to shut out all.

'Tis hard to hear the dove's wild cries of pain,
　　The hawk's beak in her heart ; 'tis hard to stay
And listen to the young lambs' moan in vain,
　　　　Their mothers torn away.

'Tis hard with wounded hands, the whole day long,
　　To strive and fail again, and always fail,
And then steal home before the vesper song
　　　　Desolate, and cold, and pale.

I have a garden all my own hard by,
　　And I have singing birds and fragrant flowers ;
In spring I set a lily pale and high
　　　　And cold, for summer hours.

A passion-flower I long since learned to love,
　　And ever kept from weeds with patient care,
And roses rich—but not the rose above
　　　　High in the cold, fine air.

The rose that always hides in blossom white
　　Such sure safe balsam for the wounded years—
Poor years ! They should be gone clean out of
　　sight,
　　　　I washed them with such tears.

Sometimes I think a whisper cometh near,
　　When every shade of gold has left the west.
Ah, me ! I wish the summer night was here,
　　　　The young lambs safe at rest.

I think, till thinking strengthens to a hope :
   That two sweet hands across a cruel tree,
Pierced through and through, high on a green hill's
      slope,
         Will bring my rose to me.

It may be many years—it may be one —
   It may be just some day, as days go by ;
But, near or far, I know that, this once done,
         I shall not fear to die ;

I shall not fear to sleep and rest unstirred,
   Or rather I shall wake to sleep no more—
To rapture sweeter than of singing bird,
         Or wave on golden shore.

THE FRIENDLESS KING.

THE good King's voice, from His Throne each day
    Came tender and low if a friend might heed ;
But His crown was wove of a thorny spray,
    His sceptre a trembling reed.

His Hands and His Feet had a crimson streak,
    And all His apparel was stained with gore ;
His face was weary, His aspect meek,
    His sad Heart lonely and sore.

For a chalice was laid near His right hand,
    With a draught that was drawn from the bitterest
       spring,
That whoever chose by His throne to stand,
    Should drink for love of the King.

And many had tasted and walked away
    Since 'twas hard and bitter as lees of gall,
The drink that the King had drunk that day
    He hung on the rood for all.

The first He called to Him were the poor ;
    Then one with the guileless heart of a child,
He saw in a white robe down at the door,
    Who emptied His cup and smiled.

Then a sad-browed woman crept softly in,
    With her vesture soiled, and her proud head low—
His sorrowful eyes saw all of her sin
    And washed her white as the snow.

Next, one who had come from a grave drew near,
    To drink of His chalice with trembling hands,
And a broken heart, from the dead so dear,
    Laid fresh in the dark grave-bands.

The white surf sobbed on the lonely shore,
    The seagulls cried where the breaker bends,
And the storm and spray swept in at the door,
    For the King who had no friends.

There was rich red wine for whoever might thirst,
    And a royal board for each honoured guest—
The poor, and the sad, and the white-robed first:
    Few heeded the King's behest.

His foes had many a dread snare laid,
    Their fierce hate breathed in every breath;
But they fell themselves on the sword's sharp blade,
    And their wounds bled fast to death.

Then the King rose up before one could call,
    From His purple throne where His courtiers stood,
And He washed their wounds, and He healed
    them all,
        In a bath of His own heart's blood.

The wild bird sang at the grey dawn's birth,
    And the moss-rose wept in the starlight dim ;
But the treasure the King prized most on earth—
    Man's heart—was closed to Him.

            ^^^^^^^^^^^^^^^^^

AT REST.

As bends a mother o'er an empty grave
    Where she had hoped her darling son might
        sleep,
    Who still must toss 'mid monsters of the deep
And slimy things that crawl beneath the wave,—
Crying : "If but the cruel waters gave
    Those poor remains, unshrouded still, to keep
    To this kind earth where I might come and weep,
And my sick soul from such wild grieving save !"

So must I murmur evermore as now,
    Still cherish long the wish I dare not name,
        So strange and sad, through all the sleepless
            night :
        That *thy* poor head were pillowed out of
            sight—
    The wrong and restless life, the slighted fame,
Forgot in the calm pallor on thy brow.

THE DEAD BIRD AND THE CHILD.

SITTING alone on the green sward there,
  Long lashes veiling downcast eye,
While small hands hide in the vesture blue—
  Little child, speak to me—tell me why.

Parting a fold in the tiny dress,
  Slowly the soft white fingers stirred,
Twisting one round the trembling lips,—
  "He died last night, my poor little bird."

Holy and strange are a young child's eyes,
  Wondering, and awed, half sad, half shy—
Gazing, you long after better things;
  Thinking, you turn away with a sigh.

Tenderly down on the green, green grass,
  Small gold wings that will fly no more;
Tremblingly, blue eyes gaze for a while,
  Then sobbing, a shower of hot tears pour.

Mournfully watching the weeping child,
  Sadly I looked on the golden wings—
Yet not for the bird, nor all for the child,
  And yet for both, and for other things.

He brought the bird when the fields were cold,
 And chill frosts lay on the branches white—
"'Twill sing," he said, " in the summer time ;"
 He said, 'twould sing—and it died last night.

I loved the boy for his mother's sake,
 I liked the bird for its low, sweet song ;
The child was dear for his winning ways,
 We reared the bird through the winter long.

Not all for the lad, nor yet for the bird,
 And still for both was I sad that day,
For I dreamt a dream of his onward path
 With bright things faded and dead on the way

Sad and solemn the church-yard lies,
 With its waving graves, like the surging sea,
Lonesomely there the white snow drifts,
 On one small mound 'neath a dark beech tree.

The white snow drifteth, the wild flowers blow,
 And winter and summer the birds sing there :
And vain was the dream I sorrowing dreamt,—
 The little child rests with the Angels fair.

A PRESENTIMENT.

SHE often told me of her early life,
And of the sweet, pale mother dead so young.
This time we stood beneath the beechen trees,
Watching the tracery 'twixt branch and leaf,
That interweaving shadowed the green grass.
A breath of wind stole from the lilies near,
And sighed a fragrant message o'er her cheek,
And as in answer, with a graceful haste,
Moving, she bent above the whispering flowers,
And stretching out a delicate, white hand,
Sought softly 'mid the stems, for one fresh bud,
That was removed a day from perfect bloom,
And swaying at her fingers' slender touch,
Slow fluttered to the earth a shower of leaves,
That should have died in perfume noons gone by.
A dreamy softness gathered in her eyes—
And something of a sadness 'round her mouth,
That held in check the smiles that should be there,
And made them the more sweet.
                She paused in dreams :
Gazing far out beyond the broken flowers,
To where the low moon shimmered in the east,
And Angels folded all the blue aside,
Forth leading slow the pensive early stars.

Half parted in a tremor yet, her lips
Sighed tenderly, at what the lilies said.
She stood as one entranced.   My sweetest friend !
Some grey clouds passing filmed all the moon ;
I watched her with a dark presentiment,
That smote the very life-strings of my heart ;
The sadness lingered still around her mouth,
And something of a trouble marked her brow,
As one who hesitates to speak a thought
He dearly loves, but which he knows full well
Must hurt the heart that ever loves him best.
" 'Tis easier to die young than old," she said.
" Yon ivy planted endmost by the wall
Has clinging tendrils few.   Wait yet awhile,
Till it has done the rounding sum of years,
And sent its life-sap branching outwards far.
From closing many graves our hearts grow damp,
And tremble ere the mattock strikes our own.
Not one grey hair will ever mock the gold
You praise amid these auburn tresses now.
Consumption kissed my mother's brow, and sealed
Its unchanged beauty, changeless evermore,
And by the reed-entangled Suir she rests,
Laid 'neath a bed of lilies and fine mould.
Yet often in that sweetest hour that falls
Scarce after nightfall, and before the dark—
Long gazing through the purple-fretted skies,
And listening 'mid the melancholy winds,
To what the dying flowers say—I start

To catch a voice that whispers strangely sweet,
And all so low, that none but me might hear—
'Tis my dead mother's voice, and well I feel
I shall die young."
               "Mary!" I cried
In anguish of reproach that jarred against
Each letter of the dear, familiar name,
So often on my lips through every hour
Of all those precious days that marked the years
Since first we two were friends.   Her head drooped
   low,
Until it met the small white hands stretched out
To soothe her face.   "Mary," I said again,
In anguish of such sudden pain as choked
All other words.   The silence smote my heart
Like that long silence that should follow soon,
And by a deep-drawn breath I knew she wept.
I thought of that strong man I saw one day,
Who unawares had walked upon a grave,
That was fresh made, and yielded to his feet;
Like him, I shuddered too, but could not weep.
A dove moaned softly in the branches near,
And sent a shower of glistening dew-drops down
Along the drooping head.   She raised her brow,
And lifted up the heavy tear-wet lids,
Slow searching for the east.   "Ah me!" she said,
" You hold the soul a poor thing if you deem
One true affection withers with the grave.
Beyond those stars the blessed ever dwell,

The friends who loved us, whom we prized and lost,
Who watch our paths with a more tender love,
Made pure from that sad taint of selfishness
That twines round things most beautiful on earth,
To soil and clog them evermore below.
Remember that I, too, made perfect there,
Will watch in love o'er you, and often come
In some such hour as this, if God permit,
To hold your lingering steps, with errands sweet,
From those dead friends that ever grow more dear.

My sweetest friend ! Four summers scarcely waned
Ere your gold hair was laid beneath the turf,
Far southwards, by the reed-entangled wave,
Leaving such memories of a holy life
As shame the lilies' lustre evermore
Near your white soul. Ah ! many hopes and years
And fairest promises have passed away,
Since that sad night we stood beneath the trees
But your true word has ever still been kept
In wiser ways than once I foolish dreamed.
Wandering alone what time the darkness falls
Athwart the twilight hills, when the sad winds
Come laden with the scent of dreaming flowers,
And, like a timid guest, the strange moon stands
Upon the farthest crystal of the skies,
I catch the spirit-music of your life,
Your youth of prayerful courage, and strong hope
And lowliness of heart—that sweetest grace

That crowned so many graces in your soul;
And, oh! with what sad eyes, grown dim with tear
I bow my head and know that you are near,
And mark the gulf that lies betwixt us two,
And think of the sweet days so long since dead.

A WISE SINGER.

A ROBIN sang a few yards from the door;
　He sang and watched the hedge and looked at me,
　Hopped round and sang, and eyed me warily.
With full reserve of better things in store,
'Twould seem he never sang enough before—
　Sang high, sang low, sang as 'twere death, had he
　Been ever once compelled to check his glee,
And yet—his song a note of sadness bore.

Perhaps to wake my pity he is fain,
　Poor bird! lest I should touch his little nest—
To please me thus he tries with sweetest strain
　For those five fledglings 'neath their mother's breast.
Or might my aching heart his song explain
And dream he sings to ease my ceaseless pain?

3

WAITING.

" WHY do you walk out there by the shore,
Reading the blue skies, watching the foam,
Chilled with the night-winds, wet with the spray ?
Come with me, poor woman, back to your home."

She looked on the waves, and looked to the sky,
And she pressed her brow with her trembling hand:

That bright star shone when my child sailed out ;
I said I would meet him here on the strand.

They tell me he's dead, but I never heed—
They speak of a wreck far out at sea ;
But what did I do to those angry waves
That they'd take my one only child from me ?

'Tis six long years, and he comes not back—
Six long, long years is my boy away—
And I watch the stars and I watch the sea,
And I wait till his ship comes, night and day.

The wild waves whisper and call his name,
And a music swells on the rising tide ;
Should you ever meet with him out beyond,
Will you say I'm waiting, the strand beside?

He has deep blue eyes, and his hair is brown,
And his smile is sweet, and his look is wild ;
Oh ! do not blame me.   Six long years gone—
And he was my one and my only child.

He loved me well, and he loved the waves,
But he loved them more, or we'd never part ;
I only smile when they say he's drowned,
For the sea came first in my poor boy's heart.

They're not so cruel, those starlit waves,
As to take and kill him, out far away :
Should you ever meet with him there beyond,
Say his mother waits through the night and day.

And they think I'm cold and lonesome here—
Walking all day by the shore so wild—
Watching the stars and watching the sea,
And waiting still for my only child.

The kind old neighbours cry for me—
They cry for the boy hid under the foam ;
I only smile when they say he's dead,
But I know that myself must soon go home.

Yet I'll never rest 'neath the cold green sod—
I said I'd wait here down on the strand ;
They must let me lie where the wild waves moan
They must make my bed in this soft, brown sand.

No mould nor worm comes here, I know,
And the waters whisper and call his name;
I can watch the seas, I can watch the sky—
I promised to meet him here when he came.

I never mind when they say he's dead,
And you'll know him yet if out there you meet—
He has dark-brown hair, and his eyes are blue,
His face is fair, and his smile is sweet.

Just say I'm growing a little tired,
And a little weak in the driving rack—
That I sometimes feel I must soon go home,
Though I thought to wait till the ship came back.

But I'll never rest by the cold green sod—
They must make my bed where the sand is piled;
Where the waters speak and the stars shine down,
I shall wait in peace for my only child.

FIRST THINGS.

THE lily is stately and fair,
   The rose is a beautiful thing,
But no flower that scents the bright air
   Is sweet as a primrose in spring.

Good deeds are not balanced by gold ;
   The friends of to-day are sincere,
But ah ! not the same as the old—
   They never can be quite as dear.

Kind words soothe an aching heart much,
   Soft hands make some weary pains go ;
But somehow we find not the touch
   Of fingers that healed long ago.

A poet sings on all the day,
   Men listen still ever athirst ;
Yet, sing he as sweet as he may,
   No songs please his heart like the first.

The green leaves are green at all time,
   But no green like the shoots of the larch ;
No voice of the summer may chime
   With the voice of the young lambs in March

All freshness and youth please the sight,
    And men ever praise the first part :
So, too, of things lovely and bright
    The *first* is most dear to God's heart.

A PROMISE.

" THERE'S not a flower in all these woodlands nigh,
    Amid the summer's grass there's not one blade,
    But when the sunshine and the glory fade,
In early leaf, or withered bloom, must die.
'Tis sweet to pull the bud ere its first sigh,
    And sweetly on our youth Death's hand is laid
    They're happy who die young," she smiled, and said
As though the grave were pleasant place to lie.
" I soon must say farewell to you, my friend,
Yet not the long farewell until life's end :—
    For here's my hand; we two will sometimes meet
In lonely pathway, or in silent glen."
    You broke your promise, yet the thought is sweet
You loved me well enough to make it then.

SCARCE an hour has passed over, Joe, and I've
    waked you up again,
With this cough, and hard gasp for breath, and the
    moaning of selfish pain ;
I count that you're watching me there, full fourteen
    months long and more ;
Oh ! the strength of man's love and the depth !
    Poor Joe ! it will all soon be o'er.

I thought that I'd die last eve—for I dreamt of the
    grave and rest,
While I slept as the red sun sank, and flooded with
    gold all the west ;
And sweet was that dream of the end, and of home,
    and the long ago,
Till, waking, I felt your hot tears, and could not but
    weep with you, Joe.

But the end and the rest must come soon ; the dark·
    ness and chill grow apace ;
Joseph, come nearer, and give me one earnest, long
    view of your face ;
Ah ! the eyes—clear, blue, and kind still—the old
    honest look on the brow ;

The sweet, firm mouth of your boyhood—there
　　seems scarce a change in you now

Since we climbed to the crane's nest, far out on the
　　old castle's height,
And waded barefoot through the brook, where the
　　speckled trout dived out of sight ;
Or chased the swift hare round and round, the
　　meadows and clover-fields through,
And you lifted me up till I reached where drooping
　　the wild cherries grew.

Ah ! there still the crane builds its nest; unaltered
　　the stream flows along—
With for ever and ever, no shadow of grief or of
　　pain in its song ;
And still, through the long summer eves, other lads
　　(like us then) are at play,
And there's health, and there's freshness and life,
　　at home in old Ireland to-day.

For 'tis June, and in sunshine the hillsides from
　　green to gold change,
While enraptured the blue mists veil jealous the
　　crest of the far mountain range ;
I know how the purple heath smiles from the depths
　　of the dry torrent's bed,
And summer winds loiter to-day, where the cows
　　to the river are led.

Dear Joe, wipe the damp from my forehead, and
    soften this hard pillow here ;
Wet my lips with the cordial.   I feel that relief
    must be near.
Oh ! how soothing a strong hand's soft touch ; how
    patient an old friend's true love !
A love such as yours, my poor Joe, has a mother's
    love only above.

Let me lie in the churchyard beyond—the corner
    that looks to the west—
Say a tired stranger pined far from Erin, and there
    do his wearied bones rest ;
And, brother, at some future day, will you go and
    bring back o'er the wave
Some shamrocks from father's green sod that will
    grow here again on my grave ?

Lift me up—I'm so weary and weak.   Ah ! once,
    Joe, in anger, I said,
My strength and my youth should not fail, and
    strange lands would yield me free bread.
Alas ! the hard words and the boasting, the fierce
    pride that kept me apart—
The crushed love, and yearning and pain, that eat
    out the life of my heart.

   *   *   *   *   *   *
Hush ! Joe, old friend—God knows what's best,
    and I'm happy even now.

Speak kind words for me to Willie, and sister Nell
    with the curly brow;
Give my heart's love to my mother—mind, say *her*
    name I breathed last;
Let her and Nellie pray for me, and forgive me all
    the past.

In the dusk of autumn evenings, when the solemn
    thoughts will rise,
When the mower's scythe is resting, and in swathes
    the damp hay lies;
And in winter by the fireside, when the wind blows
    bleak and high,
And the wild geese seek the bogland, with a home-
    less, lonely cry;

When the young lambs race at twilight, in the first
    green flush of spring,
When the children pull the primrose, and the glad
    birds build and sing;
Through the sultry summer nightfalls, when the
    dead and gone arise,
They'll weep for me then lying 'neath these strange
    Australian skies.

    *   *   *   *   *   *
You'll tell them, Joseph, how we thought to travel
    home this year,
How spring-time went and came again, and I lay
    helpless here:—

Ah ! on this bed my life's short dream comes clear
    before my sight,
So hot and restless and astray. Well, death shall
    set it right.

It seems to me astray and wrong, all wrong and
    restless and astray—
A summer morn that promised well, but ended in
    a broken day ;
Ah ! hope is false, and promise vain, and life runs
    quickly o'er—
And never now—ah ! never now, I'll see poor Erin
    more.

We'd travel westward in the spring, you'll tell them
    so we said,
And I was ill, and tidings came, the news that *he*
    was dead.
Oh, father wronged ! oh, father lost ! too late, too
    late !—since then
I'd give whole worlds to hear one word from your
    cold lips again.

Yes, I thank God, now I'm dying, ere the days of
    manhood's prime,
For, Joe, perhaps—ah, yes ! God knows, feelings
    change and hearts in time.
And when I'm gone you must be brave, nor fret
    here all alone,
For we shall meet again, old friend, where no death
    nor parting's known.

You'll dig my grave close by the hedge—where the
    winds blow from the west,
Say a stranger died from Erin, and that there he
    begged to rest :
And, brother, when in years to come, you go
    across the wave,
Send shamrocks from my father's clay to grow here
    on my grave

A MAY SONG.

Ah! is He not His Mother's Son,
  And can He but be kind and sweet?
Or could the Heart that throbbed near hers,
  With aught but mercy ever beat?

The voice that rang on Juda's air,
  And thrilled men's souls with power unknown,
And pleaded pardon on the Cross;
  Oh! had it not her every tone?

Her blood flows in each purple vein;
  Like hers, His eyes, and look, and brow—
Poor human heart, hush every fear,
  Think can He be but tender now?

It needs not May, it needs not March,
  Nor one of all the Lady-days,
December white, nor August brown,
  To fill my heart with Mary's praise.

Oh! would that heart could find fit words
  To trace the thoughts that glow within,
And tell the world of all her love,
  Through years of coldness and of sin!

It may not be, my Mother sweet,
　　These things must lie 'twixt thee and me;
Nor March, nor May, nor Lady-day,
　　It needs to fill my heart with thee.

I hold my life before my eyes,
　　And read each year that went and came,
And not a joy, or grace, or good,
　　But bears the impress of thy name.

And one hour rises from the rest—
　　Thy presence then was very near,
When hot tears fell upon thy feet
　　For things I may not speak of here.

I love the church that bears thy name,
　　The place on which thy altar's raised,
I love the Saints who wrote of thee—
　　'Tis sweet to hear our Mother praised.

And blessings on the hand that placed
　　Upon thy brow the crown loved best—
The twelve star-gems in glory bright—
　　May he in Heaven above be blest.

Oh! sweetly to my soul it comes,
　　Communion hour and visit lone,
The thought that He is Mary's Son,
　　My God, upon yon lamp-lit throne

When sorrow hides God's blessed light,
    And doubts and fears assail my mind,
I know these hands in love but strike
    That once round Mary's neck were twined.

For is He not thy own sweet Son,
    And could He be but good to me?
Nor March, nor May, nor Lady-day,
    It needs to fill my heart with thee.

FORGOTTEN.

Deep 'neath the snow-drift lying,
Out 'mid the wild winds' sighing,
In the pitying folds of the willow's shade ;
Down low where the bells come tolling,
Through the sad years onward rolling,
The dear dead faces we loved are laid.

Greener the grass is growing,
Sweeter the wild flowers blowing,
Where the worm is tangled in golden hair ;
Stronger the willows' roots are,
Richer the verdant shoots are,
Where the tired hands moulder that placed them
there.

Short was the cold regretting,
Sure is the long forgetting,
Though the dead may linger in pain below :
Piteous the earnest pleading,
And constant the interceding,
Wrung out from those patient realms of woe.

Remember the far-off sweetness
Of years that in fatal fleetness
Passed onward like golden dreams away ;
And think of the love endearing,
Of the tender words of cheering,
From the poor lips pleading in vain to-day.

Think of that light illuming,
And those fearful flames consuming
Into perfect whiteness the slightest stain ;
There helpless they wait and languish,
Outstretching in friendless anguish
The tired hands seeking for aid in vain.

From friends that were held the dearest,
From hearts that were first and nearest,
From kindred love with a love too keen.
Alas ! for the short regretting,
The long and the sure forgetting,
And the tears dried up ere the grave was green.

Ah ! how shall we hope to meet them,
In Heaven to know and greet them,
Through the long night deaf to their prayers and
cries ?
Remembering the cold neglecting,
What else can we be expecting
But to meet reproach in those gentle eyes ?

· 4

Sweet the mysterious sadness,
The strange and unearthly gladness,
That Death on each calm, white brow has set.
Ah ! the kind and the tender faces,
Laid low in forsaken places,
They are not forgetting as we forget.

SPURIOUS BLOOM.

WILD winds and storm tear down our hills in March,
Clearing their onward course as fancy suits,
Smiting the promise of the tender shoots
And all the greenness of the early larch.
Last year an apple-tree that made an arch
Across the orchard path, wrenched from the roots
Burst forth in bloom in May.   Ah! never fruits
Or soon or late 'twill bear for lips that parch.

Sweet Mother Church ! the soul cut off from thee,
Though it have spurious bloom for one brief day,
Is dead at heart as is yon prostrate tree
That blocks the path and cumbereth the ground ;
Its use is gone, its sap has ebbed away,
Its very fragrance saddens all around.

A FLOWER.

A YOUNG rose trembling in sunbeams bright
   That softly glanced through a thorny spray,
Its petals white as the morning's light,
   And no folded leaf to nurse decay.
Its petals white, and its heart deep red,
   Where the perfumed breezes sweetly sighed,
And the soft dews shed their tears o'erhead
   At the robin's plaintive trill beside.

And it brought back one, now parted long,
   In an exile sweet beyond the sea—
And a dream of song, as the memories throng,
   The young rose left since the morn with me.
With life all white, and with heart aglow
   With love for God and each parted friend,
The perfumes blow where I see thee go,
   And the Cross's shade is to the end.

A type of thee doth the white rose make,
   The fair young flower—and yet, ah! no;
For its heart will break in the fierce sun's wake
   And feebly fall to the earth below.

But thou art strong, and the years are fleet,
　And full of work to be done for God,
In burning heat, where the trembling feet
　Go bravely on where the Saviour trod.

I remember the day I saw thee last,
　And think of the years that went before ;
And tears fall fast, for the fair time past,
　And the dear friend parted evermore.
Ah ! many a flower since then has died,
　And perished many a promise fair,
A blight has sighed o'er the fresh spring-tide
　And hearts are changed by sorrow and care.

The slow years pass—and I bow my head,
　And floating by is a dream of pain—
For the summers dead, and the bright hopes fled
　That never, alas ! come back again.
I bow my head in the fading light,
　For my early friend beyond the sea
With soul as white as the young rose bright
　That sang of her in the morn to me.

I.

GoD's glory was the end of all his days,
    God's poor he held his next most tender care ;
    His life was sweet with sanctities and prayer,
His ears were closed to sounds of human praise.
His treasures were in heaven : sure fixed his gaze
    On jewelled crowns that none defiled may wear ;
    He saw the world unveiled, stripped true and
        bare,
False and deformed, with changeful hollow ways.

Too humble still to hate the thing most low—
    Its case he pitied, and well understood ;
Too noble to allow his own pure soul
    To be content with less than perfect good,
With single aim he sought a single goal—
More and more like his Master's self to grow.

II.

He made no flowery pathway for his feet,
    He tarried not in any pleasant place :
    Yet was he happy with a native grace,
God and long self-control made strangely sweet.

A frightened lamb or little child would greet
    His steps, instinctive trusting to his face;
    And thinking out your thoughts, you could not
        trace
Where love for him would highest reverence meet.

Of all you loved you'd love him far the best,
    And grieve the most for loss of his esteem—
The rare, unconsious greatness of his mind
    So won all hearts, all hearts in God to bind;
Broad, common sense was his, to weigh and test
    The gold from clay, the duty from the dream.

III.

In that fine soul no room for little things
    Was found—envy, or vain display, or pride :
    The splendour of his gifts he strove to hide,
Smiling at fame and the frail crown it brings.
He had that gentleness in strength which flings
    Round manhood such rare charm.   As ebbed
        the tide
    Of his rich life, I knelt his bed beside,
(The room that night had stir of angels' wings).

" 'Tis sweet to die as live," he softly said,
    So sweet, though few were ever loved like him,
So sweet, though few could ever love as true,
    So sweet, as all earth's sights were waning dim
And Heaven had burst on his enraptured view :
Ah ! Death indeed grows sweet since he is dead.

MOUNT MELLERAY HILLS.

I STAND alone amid the hills,
And wait the footsteps of the coming night;
There is no home, nor living thing in sight;
  No sound beside the gentle rills

That glide in through the glen below,
Close fringed with branches of the mountain fir
Which the stream breezes softly lift and stir,
  And wake to sighs for their swift flow.

Can the green grass above respire?
The sun steals downward in the lurid West,
Pausing awhile before yon topmost crest—
  A globe of living, molten fire;

Then slowly passes out of view,
Leaving a shadow to this velvet moss,
To me, and to the hills, a sense of loss,
  To the sweet skies a deeper blue.

Veiled in soft waves of silver cloud,
One peak bends eastward in the summer air:
A lonely dreamer through the noontide fair—
  Pensive and mournful 'mid a crowd.

Has there been with thee some wild strife,
O solemn hill ?   And dost thou stay apart,
To question 'neath the skies a restless heart,
    Throbbing with hot, impatient life ?

Hast thou looked forth on other hours,
When the fierce lightning's tongue shall scar thy soul,
And winds and tempests in their anger roll,
    Blasting thy green things and thy flowers ;

When the swift, early mountain bird
With cries shall drink the dew-drops from thy fruits,
And the white hare break up thy tender roots,
    And rest to feed her young unstirred ;

When the full springs that thou hast nursed,
With murmurs of farewell shall quit thy side,
To gladden and enrich strange valleys wide,
    Leaving thee evermore athirst ?

O folded peak ! O silent night !
O strong hearts bleeding on the mountain way
As sorrowful as high—too oft ye pay
    With suffering for excess of light.

O lonely hills ! O higher life !
O yearning soul ! from here to the calm skies
Is little change—to light that never dies
    Beyond all darkness, pain and strife.

THE CRY OF THE SOULS.

IN the morning,
When the pure air comes unbreathèd, and the fresh
fields lie untrod,
When the lark's song rises upward, and the wet
flowers deck the sod :
In the time of earnest praying, in the hushed and
holy morn,
Hear those voices softly pleading, hear those low
words interceding,
From the green graves lonesome lying,
Evermore in sad tones crying :
" *Have pity! you at least have pity, you my
friends!*"

In the noontide,
When the hot earth almost slumbers and the tree-
tops scarcely stir,
When the bee sleeps on the lily, and the hare pants
by the fir;
When the stream-breeze softly cools you, and the
grateful shade invites :
While the hot skies far are glowing, think of pain
no respite knowing,
And those prisoned fires appalling,
And those piteous wails still calling,
" *Have pity! you at least have pity, you my
friends!*"

In the evening,

When the long day's cares are ended, and the home-group soon shall meet,

While the silent twilight deepens and comes rest for wearied feet ;

In the time of sad remembrance, give a prayer to old friends gone,

Some regret, some feelings tender, to past days and scenes surrender ;

Let your heart with mournful greeting
Hear the sad refrain repeating,

" *Have pity! you at least have pity, you my friends !*"

In the night-time,

When the stars are set in ether, and the white moon in a cloud,

When the children's hands are folded and the golden heads are bowed ;

Tell them of that fearful burning, of those souls in tortures dire :

Let their sinless hearts adoring reach Christ's throne in sweet imploring.

By those faces lost for ever,
By those smiles to greet thee never,
By the memories of past days,
And the kindness of old ways ;
By the love in life you bore them,
And the tears in death shed o'er them,
By their words and looks in dying,
Oh ! hear those plaintive voices crying :

Have pity! you at least have pity, you my friends !"

THANKS.

I HAVE read thy poems through,
  And have paused o'er every line,
  Till a meaning half divine
From their deep-veiled beauty grew :

Till the ocean's mighty roll,
  And the solitary seas,
  In wild storms and gentle breeze,
Thrilled their glory through my soul.

I have traced upon the page,
  'Mid the flow of stately rhymes,
  Genius in the far-off times—
Deeds of soldier and of sage.

Dreams of kindred with the skies—
  Visions fair as setting sun,
  When a summer's day is done,
At thy magic strains arise.

But this simple song to-day
  Was the first to draw my tears,
  For an hour in other years,
And a hope that died away.

For a dumb and bitter grief,
  Which I thought alone was mine,
  Till it speaks in words of thine,
And finds comfort and relief.

And I thank thee from my heart,
  Though this wound must still be sore,
  Till that heart can feel no more—
Thou hast felt its keenest smart.

ST. URSULA AT THURLES.*

A CENTENARY ODE.

O HAPPY childhood's home !
The brightest of youth's dreams are linked with thee,
And though far off thy children's steps may roam,
By olive-skirted shore, or storm-tossed sea,
    Their hearts will ever tenderly
Return across the separating foam,
    To thee, their dear old home.

    As inland from the sea
Steals the soft music of the ebbing tide,
Mingling with children's voices on the lea,
Till some tired sleeper on a far hill-side
    Starts, dreaming that in meadows wide
He roams a child again : in dreams are we
    Children once more with thee.

    Once more within the fold,
Close sheltered by the mother's tender love.
Alas ! our truest and our best lie cold,
The voices that sang sweetest sing above ;
    They pined, as pined the wearied dove
For her far home, and now on harps of gold
    They play, nor e'er grow old.

*A hundred years ago Anastatia Tobin was professed in the Ursuline Order, which Nano Nagle some years earlier had introduced into Ireland. Coming from the Lee to the Suir, Sister Anastatia began in a small thatched cottage the work of education which has been carried on ever since by the Ursuline Convent of Thurles.

Not after, nor before,
The fullest life may know a day more sweet,
More blessed, than the day on which thy door
First opened to their childhood's happy feet.
    To-day, O Mother! 'tis but meet,
The children whom thy fostering bosom bore
    Should stand round thee once more.

Thou hast known toil and care,
The wine-press of self-sacrifice and pain;
But when has ever passed unheard thy prayer,
Or when were thy hands lifted up in vain?
    Has not God's strong right hand again,
And yet again, raised guides whose wisdom rare
    Kept thee intact and fair?

And such is thine these days—
With clear, calm judgment and unerring hands,
Where breakers make no head he finds safe ways,
Secure from hidden rock and treacherous sands;
    His fame is told in many lands;
But dearer is thy love—more sweet thy praise
    To him than greenest bays.

Who came in sorrow here,
To this bright home that harbours nothing sad,
Who ever came, nor found the friendship dear
Of loving hearts, by God's rich wine made glad?
    To these old walls with rose-leaves clad,
Who came when roses perished from their year,
    And missed the pitying tear?

And that quick bitter word,
(As trifling as the thistle-down wind-blown)
Whose course was seldom stayed till it had stirred
To keenest pain some heart—was here unknown ;
Here charity found one bright throne
Where its soft radiance never yet was blurred
By unkind deed or word.

There is no age for thee ;
Thine is for evermore the time of spring,
Of sweet June roses on the fragrant tree,
The time of violets and first blossoming,
The time young swallows learn to sing.
O happy time ! O days too fast to flee !
O sweet, sad memory !

Thine are the opening leaves,
With their veined spears of tender, sheltered green
Thine is the seed-time.   In the day for sheaves
The Master's eyes will note what work has been ;
Thy children in far lands are seen
Countless and bright, as stars in harvest-eves,
Thine are their garnered sheaves.

O happy home ! O friends !
Good work well done lies marked in gold behind,
Good work to do each hour, each moment sends ;
Let high security for Heaven still bind
Friendship and work as with one mind
And happiness that charity attends,
To full and perfect ends.

ALONE.

Eagle, dost thou shrink in fear,
　　When the lightnings flash at night,
　　Round thy bare and dizzy height,
And the winds roar wild and drear ?

Does thy proud heart feel alone
　　When the pale clouds robe the sky—
　　When in crowds the small birds fly,
And the gray dawn chills thy throne ?

Mountain-peaks that upward rise,
　　Near, yet ever parted far,
　　Parted, as estranged hearts are—
Separate, ye must seek the skies.

When the valleys smile in gold,
　　And each shaded glen below
　　Bursts in flower at summer's glow,
Ye must bear the white snow's cold.

Soaring heart and gifted mind,
　　You too should your dreamings wean
　　On no sympathy to lean,
No soul like your own to find.

Quick to read, where hearts are shown—
　　You must find half life is vain,
　　Bear alas ! far keener pain,
Suffer, think, and dream alone.

*A POET.**

I HAD once a summer dream,
 And I saw the Poets stand
 On a far-off mountain land,
Where the purple glories gleam.

Traced upon each sunlit face,
 Underneath the crown of green,
 There were paths where tears had been,
Which no glories could efface.

But I marked, with keener pain,
 Those most gifted of that throng
 Weaving sin in sweetest song,
Poisoning each fairest strain.

And I cried : "Do angels sigh
 Over genius so ill spent ?
 Does the great, good God repent
Giving man a gift so high ?"

Then a spirit bright and fair
 Bore within his hands a lyre
 Of celestial birth and fire,
Through the hushed and solemn air,

*Aubrey de Vere.

To await a human voice—
 One such strong sweet rush of words,
 As should thrill its silent chords
To all meanings pure and choice :

One such passionate white heart,
 As should breathe among its strings
 Of divine and noble things
With a full and perfect art.

Soaring sometimes out of sight,
 Seeking 'mid each distant star
 Their own level swift and far,
Higher fancies take their flight.

Till a listless gazer cries,
 " I have lost the Poet's thought ;
 It was cold and finely wrought,
And has gone beyond the skies."

No, not cold, but only high—
 Always tender, high, and grand—
 For one line traced by thy hand,
Never need God's angels sigh.

Painting on a solemn page
 All the martyr's awful strife,
 Telling of a nobler life
To a selfish worldly age ;

Weaving sad pathetic song
   O'er the commonplace, dark days,
   O'er the friendless, lonely ways,
Where Christ's poor unheeded throng.

Thou hast bound e'en famine dread
   In such music sweet and deep,
   That men read and pause to weep,
Envying the sainted dead.

Thine has been a glorious part—
   Poet dreaming through the May,
   Singing through the golden day
With a passionate, white heart.

Round thy proud, poetic name,
   Round each full majestic rhyme,
   Men shall gather through all time,
With the praise of deathless fame.

CONSTANT.

I.

SINCE cold my precious singing bird lay there,
    I want no bird of sweeter song instead ;
    No second dog replaced the small friend dead,
That loved me well through good and evil fare.
I nursed a strange plant once with time and care,
    A thing of fragrant bloom and golden head,
    "Its delicate grace," a dear voice dream-like
      said,
" Has breath of olive woods and south-warm air."

Since then the roses bloomed and died three times,
    Unmarked by me who rear no flower again ;
Kind voices blame that I but catch sad chimes
Of death bells ringing through the patient years,—
Past any gentlest face, but see through tears
    A face more dear for death, more sweet for pain.

II.

I prize no aftermath in glen or wold,
    No grasses 'mid brown stubble all alive
    With early winter birds that scream and thrive.
I want no second summer's promised gold.

Dearer familiar paths I took of old,
  Through meads thick-set with flowers for honied
    hive ;
  Dearer remembrances that must survive
All change, to me more dear a hundred-fold

The hopes, the friends, the days for ever passed,
  The white sails set, the ocean wide before.
No venture now on any seas I cast,
No wreck provide for second surf-beat shore,
To one heart, cold and still, my heart clings fast,
  My hands but dead hands clasp for evermore.

TO ALICE.

A CLUSTER of violets deep in the shade,
   A tremble of green on the woodbine near,
And a sweet sound made in a lonely glade,
   By a rippling streamlet low and clear.
Not a voice around of a living thing,
   Save mine, and the birds that flock in the trees
With a farewell ring, in the notes they sing,
   Ere they spread their wings for the distant seas.

Will they pass thy home in their flight away?
   Will their song as they soar in the clouds above,
To thy true heart say, as to mine to-day—
   That 'tis hard to part with the things we love?
I know thee happy, and well, and strong,
   With a thirst for pain in the brave, deep heart;
Yet the memories throng, from the years along,
   And I sigh to-day, we are far apart.

I muse on the battle brave you fought,
   With affections deep and a spirit high;
And the soaring thought, that was gently brought
   Through the daily life, to itself to die.
Like one for whom love has made all sweet,
   As the rich heart gives, with a smile you gave;
And but thought it meet, to lay at His feet,
   Each thing that was dear till beyond the grave.

The days and the hours are with good things rife ;
  And you gave up much, and you gave up all,
When the young heart's strife, in the earlier life,
  Kept never a thing from the Lord's low call.
Midst the holy called to a holier height :
  Very near to Him on the Calvary way ;
Oh ! your soul is bright, in the angels' sight,
  With the beauty of sacrifice to-day.

Do you remember you sent home here
  A crucifix once as a gift to me ?
It has grown more dear, from each passing year,
  And its sermons sweet of God and of thee :
Athirst for the cross, and with love on fire,
  And holy and happy as I might will—
Yet I know you require, with the heart's desire,
  To work, and to suffer, and love more still.

Sweet are the violets hid in the ground,
  Tender the green on the woodbine spray,
And the rippling sound of the waters round,
  And the birds' farewell on their flight away :
And I stand and think of the distant sea,
  And my sad heart asks as they sing above,
Will they say to thee, as they say to me,
  That 'tis hard to part with the things we love ?

THEY HAVE TAKEN AWAY MY LORD.

Now the lights are out, and the crowd is gone,
　　And the organ hushed in a tender wail ;
And the pensive shades from the east creep on
　　Through the Gothic arch and the marble rail ;
They creep and they pause by the empty shrine,
　　And the unlit lamp, and the open door,
Where the clusters green, and the rosebuds pine
　　And the soft leaves fall to the crimson floor.

Why kneel I to stay while the rest depart,
　　And only the incense lingereth near,
With a prayerless voice, and a hungry heart,
　　And a love that dareth not love through fear ?
Ah ! He was there and they bore Him away,
　　And the white-stoled priest left the door ajar ;
And my sorrow waked, and I kneel and stay,
　　When the rest all go to their homes afar.

It waked and wailed on the music's tone,
　　And it cried out strong when the Lord was gone
And I list in fear to its troubled moan,
　　And I trembling wait till a calm comes on.

Ah ! the once bright hope that grew pale and died,
　When I never grieved in the morning hour—
And I came at noon, and I wept and cried,
　Till it started up with remorseless power.

Oh ! the hope that's dead, and the grief that slept,
　Till it waked just now with a thrill of pain ;
And the longing years, and the vigils kept,
　And the buried joy, and the prayers all vain.
Oh ! the deepening shades, and the clouded heart,
　And the light that steals from the west afar ;
And the Virgin's tenderer look apart,
　And the altar lone, and the door ajar.

Will a sorrow speak though the voice is low,
　And hardly a word or a prayer can say ?
Will it reach His ears in its 'plaining woe,
　Where anointed hands have hid Him away ?
Will She not whisper a pleading word,
　His mother and mine with the tender brow ?
His mother and mine !　Oh ! pardon, Lord !
　For my sorrow but waked and wailed just now.

Yet the night will pass, and with morning's light
　They'll leave Him here in His home once more ;
'Mid the tinkling bells and the tapers bright,
　And the crowd that knelt by His prison door.

But this thing shall stay like a spirit grieved,
   And never a morrow or sunshine feel,
Till the last pulse beat, and the sigh be heaved,
   And the darkness grow, and the death-tear steal.

" May His will be done," now I murmur low,
   "Though it seemeth harsh in its stern decree
Let this trouble stay since He wills it so ;
   One day I shall know it was good for me."
With a mournful grace doth the day depart,
   While the slow shades darken the aisles around
And the sorrow sleepeth now in my heart,
   Till it start again at a sight or sound.

A LIFE'S SEASONS.

In the Spring-time,
Ben, the youngest, and the dearest,
  Praying at his mother's side,
Running joyous all her errands,
  Playing with her seek-and-hide ;
Crying when she looked aweary,
  And a shade was on her brow,
In the spring-time, when the ash-leaves,
  Hid upon the mourning bough.

In the Summer,
Ben, the fairest and the gayest,
  Straying by a foreign shore,
Spending all his child's rich portion,
  Idols bowing down before ;
And his mother's heart was breaking,
  And her smile was seldom seen,
And they laid her 'neath the daisies,
  When the berries yet were green.

In the Autumn,
Ben, the saddened and the altered,
  Pining in a foreign land,
Heard his mother's voice of spring-time,
  Hungered for her tender hand.

And her eyes were ever on him,
　Through the night hours, in the morn,
And he came across the ocean,
　When the sloe grew on the thorn.

　In the Winter,
Ben, the contrite and the weary,
　Kneeling at his mother's grave
Praying God and her for pardon :
　Yielding back the life God gave ;
And his cheek was thin and pallid,
　And his eyes were strange and bright
And they laid him by his mother,
　Ere the snowdrop came in sight.

WHAT shall I do when the hour comes to part
  When I hear the train whistle and see the boat
    lying
Close by in the harbour just ready to start,
  With women all sobbing and strong men a-crying?
Oh ! what shall I do with the break at my heart?
Can I live to return and see you depart ?

" But I'll send you home money, I'll win for you
    gold,
  I'll work and I'll toil when the rest are all sleeping,
And I'll sail back again when you're growing too
    old ;
  I'll sail back to nurse you—then, mother, cease
    weeping.
You can soon pay the rent and sit in from the cold,
I have youth, I have health, and work's plenty,
    I'm told."

Ah ! but money and gold cannot heal a heart-sore :
  I'd rather have hunger and you by my side there,
I'd rather no fire and the snow at my door,
  I'd rather no roof but the skies and have died
    there.
How happy, mavrone, with the child that I bore,
With the angels beside me, the graveyard before !

" But want is a tyrant, sweet mother," she said—
 "If I saw you hungry, if I saw you lying,
With the chill on your brow and the gray on your
    head,
  Out there by the roadside and sickening and
    dying,
And I had no money to buy for you bread,
I'd die ere you died, I'd be laid by you dead."

Then go, and God bless you—aye, go, in God's
    name,
  The rent and the food I'll be soon past requiring ;
But you'll sail back again, you must sail all the same,
  'Tis a wish that I have, 'tis a thing I'm desiring—
(Nay, child, do not weep), tell the neighbours you
    came
Just to kneel 'mid the shamrocks and whisper my
    name.

How fair is the earth on this summer night,
　　With the silver veil o'er the drooping flowers,
And the deep-blue sky, where the far stars bright
　　Look solemnly down through the passing hours.
There is not a sound in the city now ;
　　But to-night I know there's no sleep for me—
The birds are at rest on the pale hill's brow,
　　As I sit with your letter here on my knee.

I seek not to trace one beautiful word,
　　For I read them all by the bright noon light,
And my heart at a touch of yours has stirred,
　　And my soul is strangely moved to-night.
I hear the moan of the distant sea—
　　Like a thing with itself all the hours at strife—
Oh ! the years and the sea are a mystery,
　　And a solemn thing is a human life.

　　is not the words that you wrote alone :
　　Another might write them, and I not mind :
Nor the memories sweet of the days long flown,
　　Of the old dear face, and the low voice kind.
'Tis the life that has lived every word you spoke—
　　'Tis the struggle gained with a strong young heart,

That bled in the strife till it nearly broke,
    When the Lord's voice called to the better part.

The soft June winds are sighing away
    O'er the beautiful earth and the drooping flowers ;
And the city sleeps in its mist of gray,
    And my soul cries out for the vanished hours,
For the wasted gifts, and the lost youth bright,
    For what might have been, and what now.—Ah, me !
There is music sad in the air to-night,
    And Life and its dreams are a mystery.

I see the path that your feet have trod,
    O'er the thorny way with a trustful fear—
The sight most dear in the eyes of God—
    A white soul joyful on Calvary here.
There's not a sound in the hushed midnight,
    Not a withered leaf, or a restless bird ;
And the far stars shine with a burning light,
    And the depths of my soul are strangely stirred.

By your life's clear light I have read my life,
    And a vision of failure the contrast brings ;
Yet, thank God, for your higher, nobler strife,
    For the holier ways, and the better things.
And sobbing low, like a heart in pain,
    In the far-off distance I hear the sea ;
And the soft June winds bear a saddened strain,
    As I sit with your letter here on my knee.

ON THE MOUNT.

"And they sat down and watched him."—*Matt.* xxvi. 36.

I REST my face upon my hands,
　And lay the sacred scroll aside,
And let my wandering thoughts awhile
　Rest on my Saviour crucified—
Trying to bring with love and pain
The scene of Calvary back again.

I follow through that awful day,
　And scarce less awful night before,
Behold Him mocked, and bruised, and torn
　Till hell can add no torture more :
I see its rage loosed on Him then—
His Father's wrath, the sins of men.

The worn-out lash, the clotted cloak,
　The red pool in the judgment hall,
Where flowed the Blood from veins laid bare,
　Besprinkling pillar, steps, and all :
I see the reed and thorny crown,
And mark the crimson drops flow down.

Fixed to a cross with three rough nails,
   That fair and fatal town outside,
While skies are black at midnoon hour,
   And from the grave pale shadows glide;
Suspended 'mid the trembling air,
They sat them down and watched Him there

The Mother stands in speechless woe,
   Suffering each pang with keener dart;
The thorny crown, the iron spikes,
   Pierce sharper through her broken heart
His low " I thirst " falls on her ear,
While gloating eyes still watch Him near.

That face so ever like to hers
   Is strangely beautiful e'en now,
As tremblingly the shade of Death
   Flits o'er the Lord of Life's pale brow.
His plaintive moan steals on the air,
And cruel hearts still watch Him there.

Oh ! tremble, sorrow-heaving earth,
   And hide thy face, shamed sun, the more,
And Magdalen and John, press close
   To her who stands that cross before—
On fire with pain, one tortured thrill—
Oh ! woe and grief ! they watch Him still.

I cry: My Mother ! give me tears,
   And heart with love and sorrow rife,

For Him and thee that fearful day,
   And for my own poor sinful life ;
Touch thou my soul with Pity's power
That I may weep with thee this hour.

Oh ! let me learn for Christ's dear sake
   To bear in silence lesser pain,
And with my God all desolate
   To suffer meekly, nor complain.
And thou wilt teach and be my guide,
Sweet Mother of the Crucified !

OUR EMIGRANTS.

YE wander far and far,
By many a distant star,
　　By many an olive shore.
The swallows come and go,
　And come again with May ;
The tide-waves ebb and flow,
　　The brown hair turns to gray,
　　　But ye come back no more.

Ye eat the exile's bread,
As bitter-hard as lead,
　　Ye walk a way apart.
Change follows swift on change ;
　The faces that ye meet
Are cold and hard and strange—
　　Through city and through street
　　　Ye bear the homeless heart.

Why must ye go away
In hundreds every day,
　　As from a plague ye fled ?—

O young man, maid, and child
  Ye leave a fertile soil,
A climate soft and mild,
    A land to pay all toil,
      A land of glorious dead.

The savage rears her child,
And in the forests wild
      Finds all their need demands;
But from a verdant shore,
    And from the hills ye love,
Ye rush forth evermore,
      While angels weep above—
        Sad exiles in all lands.

Ye cut the quinine wood,
Where once the red man stood,
      Where dwells the humming bird;
But far and far away,
    Across the deep green sea,
Throughout the night and day,
      Your thoughts for ever flee,
        In love that finds no word.

Ye dig the yellow gold
From streams of wealth untold,
      Through weary, painful hours:
Oh! leave it where it lies,
    Just standing as it stood,

For to our aching eyes
　　It bears a mark of blood—
　　　　Of your life's blood and ours.

'Tis bought with too much pain,
It has a crimson stain,
　　　　The red sweat of your hearts ;
Ye give it full and free,
　　Ye eat the bitter bread,
To keep the old roof-tree
　　Above the bent, gray head,
　　　　That to the grave departs.

Oh ! come to us once more,
Come from the olive shore,
　　　　Across the salt-sea foam ;
We'd rather than the gold
　　That ye were with us here ;
We'd suffer want and cold,
　　Nor shed a single tear,
　　　　If ye were but at home.

AT THE SUNSET.

LET us go to the upland shade awhile,
  As the sun sinks down in the crimson west,
See ! the fields are lit with a tender smile,
  And the cattle deep in the cool grass rest ;
I shall seek this place in the future years,
  I shall know this hour when you're far away ;
Twill be time enough for my grief and tears,
  And I could not weep if I would to-day.

How your hot hand trembles ! your face is white,
  And your eyes are strange with the fevered pain,
Like the stars we watched on a late spring's night
  When the death-frost swept over hill and plain :
How the vesper bell thrills the evening air,
  And the silence deepens far and wide !
Our kindred rest in the graveyard there,
  By the tall church tower on the green hill side.

Tis hard to live, and 'tis hard to die—
  May no troubled dreams on those sleepers break !
God's time is best, and the years go by,
  Yet I know which choice in this hour I'd take.
I remember you as you were a child,
  I can picture since how each bright year ranged,
I can see you young, and glad, and wild,
  I may never know you old or changed.

'Tis a voice of power that has bid you rise,
   And forget your home and your father's land,
To live and die 'neath the stranger's skies,
   And to never clasp but the stranger's hand ;
But pain may wait on the unborn years,
   Since pain is best for a human soul,
And the path you chose may be dim from tears,
   When ten thousand waves will between us roll.

Do you think of a morning long ago,
   When the young larks fled through the fields
     away ?
Just a bluer sky and a warmer glow,
   And they took their flight in the bright June
     day,
With a stronger beat in each parting wing,
   With a joyful tremor they went. Ah ! me—
But the heart of man is a weary thing,
   And the ways of God are a mystery.

Will you stand by the seas and behold this place
   As I shall stand when you're far away ?
I shall stand in dreams and recall your face,
   As white and strange as it looks to-day.
Will your strong heart pine on the stranger's
    shore ?
   Will your tears flow yet for the friends you
     leave ?
Will you weep for home, should your heart grow
    sore ?
   Will you weep for me, should you learn to grieve ?

REGRETS.

I WISH the swallows never came
   'Mid summer roses flitting :
Red roses with their hearts aflame,
White lilies that have never found a name
   Their fragrant sweetness fitting.

They leave me when the summer's dead,
   When all things fair are dying ;
They glance and sing, light wings wide spread,
White-breasted, happy, shooting high o'er head,
   From me, from winter flying.

To-day they muster to depart :
   Where will they sing to-morrow ?
To-night when cold, wan moonbeams dart,
The rose will weep, the lily break her heart,
   For swallows gone, for sorrow.

I think upon that sweet spring day,
   I heard the first lamb bleating ;
I think when swallows came in May—
I weep for all the music passed away,
   For happiness too fleeting.

Now lambs are moaning since the noon,
   Within the green fold lying;
A few weeks hence—in one full moon,
They will forget their mothers just so soon,
   Nor pain me with their crying.

Sweet summer days will come once more,
   Dark swallows will be singing,
Red roses blossom as before,
White lilies dream beside the open door,
   Upwards their fragrance flinging.

But not for me, oh! not for me
   These golden days are keeping :
My birds lie drowned in the wild sea,
My flower and root lie perished in the lea ;
   There's nought for me but weeping.

The lambs will soon forget and rest,
   Forget and cease complaining,
And on the green earth's kindly breast
Could I forget, and sleep, sleep sound—'twere best—
   Sleep long, from tears refraining.

I.

We parted on a grey October morn,
　Sad roses lingering here and there fell fast,
　Whilst autumn sighed through every fitful blast,
For weeping bough, and bleak, deserted thorn.
When summer's bloom lay low, dank, and forlorn,
　Thy graves, O earth! were crowding thick and
　　fast
　(Sometime I'll find a grave with thee at last,
A better time than that when I was born).

We parted in the autumn cold and grey,
　Since then I count the slow days one by one;
　There's nothing left to me beneath the sun—
When we may meet again I cannot say:
　I count the days—but who would count the
　　years,
　With their wild rain of heart's blood and of
　　tears?

II.

If I could but have gone and he should stay!
　Ah me! if I might die in his dear place!
　He leaned on God alone—he rich in grace;
I needed God and him. Now each dark day

Alone and heart-sick, 'mid chill shadows grey,
  I dream, when Death and I stand face to face—
  For, swift or slow, Death always wins the race—
Will he draw near to light the sunless way?

My God! was this poor heart as so much gold
  That you should break, and change in seething
    fire?
But half 'twas yours, I know. See, Lord, to-day
  There's none but you. (Ah! my loved dead lie
    cold
And far.) See, Lord, this heart you so desire
  Is yours alone. Then change to gold its clay

THE HEART OF HEARTS.

God's Sacred Heart—oh! sweetest words
That ever waked the slumbering chords
   Of music in a human heart;
More tender than the breeze that floats
And sighs amid the wind-harp's notes,
   When evening's lonely steps depart.

More soft than tones of earthly love,
Or mellow voice of plaintive dove,
   Amidst the quiet summer trees;
More gladdening to the spirit's ear
Than songs that soothe, and words that cheer
   Or message from the parting seas.

The Heart that loved us first and best,
And showed its depth by such fierce test,
   Our cold forgetful hearts to move:
One tear God's anger had appeased,
One sigh man's fearful doom released,
   Yet He would die, His love to prove.

Amidst men's sons most fair He stood,
Alone unselfish, noble, good,
   The friendless and the sinner's friend.

The bruisèd reed He would not break,
The outcast leper not forsake,
 Nor little children from Him send.

The red beads scar His brow these days,
As when the Paschal moon's white rays
 Shone round Him in His agony.
For those He trusted faithless proved,
And wounds are made by hands that loved,
 And last and least of all is He.

We lavish love for trivial claim,
But yesterday, to-day the same,
 For Him alone there's none to spare
Neglected, slighted, and forgot,
His pleading low still answered not
 Few grieve for Him, for Him few care.

Down beside a golden iris knelt a fair boy on the
    ground,
Where the mint flung up its incense, and the cow-
    slips drooped around;
" Mother Mary," softly singing in a child's voice
    low and clear,
And the summer winds were sighing, and the glad
    birds warbling near.

Came his father there to seek him in the evening
    while he prayed,
And the sight was very tender, and his quiet foot-
    steps stayed;
Long he watched the small head bending, heard
    the glad birds warbling wild,
While " Mother Mary," softly prays he, "guard my
    holy, sinless child."

Years went by and brought their changes, twenty
    summers bright and fair,
Brought the father care and sorrow, blighted hopes
    and silver hair;

And the iris flags were waving, and the winds made
    music low ;
But—where's he who knelt beside them, knelt and
    prayed there long ago ?

Still the purple mint is blooming, and rich perfume
    upward sends,
And the chaliced iris glowing, and the cowslip
    graceful bends,
And the glad birds still are singing, and an old man
    sad and mild
Comes at evening, and he murmurs, "O my child!
    my poor lost child !"

No, not lost, poor weary father ! though he wan
    dered far away
Since you prayed for him that evening, since he
    sang that sweet child-lay ;
Kneeling at our Lady's altar, weeping in a distant
    place—
In this hour your boy is holy, beautified anew in
    grace.

Once again the picture changes, and the young
    man seeks the old,
And with claspèd hands before him, kneels as when
    his prayers he told ;
"O my father, pity ! pardon !" humbled, broken,
    whispers he,
While the father weeping murmurs, "Mother Mary,
    thanks to thee !"

MAGDALEN.

I.—HER TEARS.

TEARS, tears—the ceaseless language of her heart,
  That passionate poor heart the Saviour breaks,
  And, filling with His blessed sorrow, takes
All that is evil from, with tender art.
They mingle with the oil and gums, they dart
  In showers o'er His feet, until she makes
  Of that rich gold 'neath which her forehead aches
A veil to dry them ere she will depart.

'Tis hard to be a saint.   It needs sweet grace
  And humblest trust and sacrifice and pain,
    The prayers and blood and strivings of a life.
    But Mary's deeper love forgets all strife—
  Forgets herself, her shame, her loss, her gain
Weeping before the sadness of *His* face.

II.—" I WILL TAKE HIM AWAY."

Weeping, she humbly stands without the door,
  Nor enters there—though she would deem it
    sweet
  To kiss the precious stones that kissed His feet
And, kneeling, every crimson stain adore.

Her soul is sick with fear, her heart is sore,
   Her depth of desolation is complete :
   She sees the empty tomb—*His* last retreat
Who never claimed a place to rest before.

Poor, loving heart !—" I will take Him away ?"
   Death's weight is heavy on His pallid brow ;
'Tis three-and-thirty summers since He lay
   Within His mother's arms—and trembling now,
And weak from grief—faint, worn in every sense,
You dream your love gives strength to bear Him
    hence !

AN AUTUMN MEMORY.

THE silver mists break o'er the far hills away ;
  The sunbeams of autumn shine down clear and
    cold ;
The dark bent droops sad by the lone moor to-day,
  Where the wild winter bird-notes are plaintively
    told.
The faded leaves seek in the cold earth a grave,
  Where the sweet-briar hangeth, all robed in deep
    red,
The plumes of the alder in rich sables wave
  Where November winds mourn for the bright
    Summer dead.

The tassels of clover the tired reaper slays ;
  The hazel-tree bends with its full pendants
    brown,
The bloom lingers still where the wild woodbine
    stays,
  From its fair sister-flowers, a-buried far down.
The white snow will come yet—the pure and white
    snow—
  To nurture the petals asleep in the ground,'
And spring-days will dawn, and the spring breezes
    blow,
  And fresh things and lovely will start up around.

The autumn awakens a dream in the heart,
  When November winds mourn for the bloom on
    the lea ;
From time and from distance a sad dream will
    start—
  The sound of a parting, the sob of the sea.
Like passionate echoes that Song wrings from pain,
  The memories that cry from that day by the
    shore,
Where brave ships awaited the will of the main,
  And one sailed to East, to return never more.

Oh ! if for an absence our hearts only bled,
  The clasp of a hand that was tender and true,
The tones of a voice, and the kind words once
    said,
  The sound of a footstep our ears full well knew !
Though absence is grief, and the dead have our
    tears,
  Yet life may flow smooth 'neath a yet keener
    pain ;
Alas ! for the hope that dropped out from the years,
  Alas! for the want and regret that remain.

Oh the strength of the billows, the beauty and
    pride !
  When waves broke in sorrow, as seemed they
    that day,
For brave ships departing to purple seas wide,
  Where angry white mountains gaped hungry
    away.

Oh ! the fall of the leaf-time, far off from the shore,
　The hope that for ever died out by the sea,
The shadows that stay to depart never more,
　When November winds mourn for the bloom on
　　the lea.

ON THE ROCKS.

THERE'S scarce a breath around the green hill sides,
    And scarce a breeze blows o'er the sultry sea ;
From one small boat that through the water glides
    A song in foreign tongue steals up to me :
The voice sounds sweet, though somewhat sad
      and deep,
    Mingled with moaning waves that rush along,
And still a low, complaining chorus keep,
    Like dreams, or like old memories through a
    dreamer's song.

Great peaks of cliff loom eastward bare and brown,
    And make this quiet beach and sheltered seat
Seem more remote :—long surges rise, and drown
    The sound of busy mart, and crowded street :
On restless wings the swift, white sea-birds fly,
    (The wing so tame and tender for its nest),
Nor ever cease that strange, half-painful cry,
    O'er yellow sands, or on the billow's topmost
    crest.

I see one cloud gold-tinged—but one—to-day,
    Slow sailing westward to the horizon's verge ;
A moment's pause :—farewell—and then away
    To die where sea and sun in glory merge ;

Farewell, gold cloud :—lost cloud, you leave behind
  One heart more grave ; the sea grows dark—and I
Stand filled with sadness vague and undefined,
  Yearning for what lives not on ocean, earth, or
    sky.

The fishing boats their white sails homeward bend,
  Proud, foreign flags from tall masts deck the bay,
Two stately ships far outward slowly wend
  O'er trackless wastes to distant ports away ;
Untired the sea-bird's restless wing goes by,
  Back from the shore rush beaten waves in fear
Pale evening shadows fleck the cloudless sky,
  And still the plaintive music softly steals up here

A Grecian pennant flutters down below,
  With oars scarce stirred the sailor moves along,
And in a voice appealing, young, and low,
  Thrills all the air with sound of mournful song
Poor lad ! is his heart chased with dreams like
    mine ?
  Lives he once more the far-off, careless days,
By white-trunked palm, by olive grove and pine,
  'Mid lands of sun and bloom, and friends with
    warm and gentle ways?

Feels he to-day the storm that tore his breast,
  Whilst wild waves chant the same bewitching
    strain,
To lure his heart from all it loved the best,
  His pulse to thrill for dangers o'er the main ?

Or does he hear his mother's broken voice,
   Or see his father's nerveless, trembling hands,
Outstretched to save him from that wayward choice
   Of ocean's roar, of storm-tossed seas, and un-
      known lands?

Be still, wild waves! moan not, crushed by the tide;
   Hush, sailor-boy! why sing so sad of home?
Cold seas, laugh out! you fright me dark and wide;
   White bird, have peace! rest still on sand or
      foam:
Ah me! the wave repulsed finds golden shore,
   By lands of spice and palm, by coral isles;
The ship-boy hears his mother's voice once more;
   The sea-bird sleeps, though tempests shriek and
      wreck for miles.

Kind nature keeps a respite and a change
   On her broad breast for all, she mocks
At none, nor home-sick boy, nor sea-bird strange,
   Nor wild waves thundering round the riven rocks:
And thou, sad heart! dream-haunted, restless, wild,
   Sick with regrets that slumber not nor cease.
Look back, long winters past seem short and mild,
   Come hail, come frost, strange heart! the night
      comes soon, and peace.

REVERIES.

Tis June in tender moonlight skies,
  'Tis twilight in this cool retreat,
  Where bending birch and osier meet
O er leaves whose greenness never dies.

The heron's favourite haunt is here,
  Her foot is in the brook each day ;
  Through long, damp swathes of new-mown hay,
A hundred sweet, dead flowers appear.

On hill sides far the dry heath lights,
  Where silver waves of fire float low,
  Here happy children to and fro
With bare feet wade these moonlight nights.

On earth and sky and far-off sea,
  It is a lovely tender hour :
  Sweet Virgin, crowned with gracious power,
To-night in Heaven what must it be !

This English speech is hard and cold,
  Would I might weave here at your feet,
  In mine own language soft and sweet,
A song that half my love might hold !

But that sweet tongue is well-nigh dead,
  And with my race is scattered far :
  Your altars stand 'neath any star,
Where Irish hearts have loved and bled.

Ah ! strange to me my father's tongue,
  And wide my people dwell apart :
  The song is from a Celtic heart
Although in alien English sung.

I knelt in a Cathedral aisle,
  A June eve past, before your throne,—
  Knelt long, scarce praying, and alone,
The organ pleading sad the while.

I could not pray, but tears came fast,
  Each sighing note was fraught with pain,
  And round through every mournful strain
Rushed memories from a sorrow past.

And thoughts that could but speak in tears,
  And grateful love that found no word
  Went out in chords that waked, and stirred,
And trembled, through the far-off years.

The aid oft sought and oftener given,
  With full and prompt and generous hand,
  Though I should fail to understand
That pain must guard the path to Heaven.

Ah! cold this song I sing for you,
　　My Mother sweet, God's Mother dear;
　　What other friend could be so near,
So tender, patient, kind, and true?

Beyond the skies and planets fair,
　　Beyond the countless seraph throng,
　　Beyond the arch-angelic song,
You listen for the sinner's prayer.

Your throne is near God's Throne above,
　　Full mercy by the Judgment place;
　　When I shall stand before His face,
My dearest hope is in your love.

But ah! there may be many a day
　　Between to-night and my last breath:
　　Doubt and temptation, pain and death,
A long, and hard, and unknown way.

The fragrant blossoms deck the grass
　　The mower laid in damp swathes low;
　　Sweet Mother, may my life shine so
When Death's strong scythe o'er me shall pass;

With some fair bloom that you may prize,
　　Some passion-flower or violet sweet,
　　Or lilies to lay at your feet
Beyond those tender moonlight skies.

MARY.

A FADED leaf—some kind words traced
  By hands long mouldering in the clay,
And strangely there arises here
  A sweet familiar face to-day.
A glad and fair and youthful face,
  With low, arched brow and earnest eyes,
In whose clear depths forever dwelt
  The tender calm of summer skies.

Across the long and changeful years,
  It takes my heart with yearning pain,
To hours long past, and friends long gone,
  To things that may not be again.
Through changeful years, with changeless love,
  My heart returns to those days past—
And, Mary, to that parting hour,
  We stood beside the river last.

We watched the tired sun climb the west,
  And bathe in crimson hill and town,
And sad it seemed that we should part,
  Before that sun again went down ;
The bridge was there with wallflower grown
  In grasses deep the speedwell grew,
Beside us, o'er the winding Suir,
  The songless waterbirds swift flew.

We waited while the stars stole out,
   And one by one in glory shone,
Some shone and twinkled and appeared
   Like children's eyes when sleep comes on :
Our hearts were sad, were vaguely glad,
   For many a past and coming year,
For hopes that had scarce birth or death,
   For dreams—for something far or near ;

We knew not what : when we shall meet
   Where you are gone, all will be known,
Still most unlike—you went, I stayed—
   With death and tears familiar grown.
You sleep in peace beside the Suir
   Long miles away, yet still are near ;
Seas may divide, but death parts not—
   I speak ; and, Mary, you can hear.

In hours of pain you tried to write,
   Till pen from wasted fingers dropped :
You spoke of heaven, you spoke of peace,
   Of love unchanged—and there you stopped.
Grief is but selfish, Love is weak,
   I placed that note with tears away ;
I know you are with God—and still
   I dare not read it o'er to-day.

Ah, Mary! you were good and true,
   As only hearts like yours can be—
Unselfish, gentle, shy, and kind,
   All sweetness and humility.

You held yourself the least of all,
  You ever chose the lowest place ;
They should grow violets at your feet,
  Grow lilies o'er your heart and face.

O voice for ever silent now !
  O face so beautiful this hour !
O eyes where stayed the calm of Heaven
  Ye hold me with a tender power.
And like the grace that grows from prayer,
  A sweetness lingers round these dreams,
My hardness takes your softer ways—
  My life from yours scarce parted seems.

CHANGES.

I.

Summer has bloom, and Autumn fruit, and Spring
Fresh, fragrant buds, wild winds, and spangling
frost,
Soft, woolly nests in rocking elm boughs tossed,
Or 'mid gold furze where stays the linnet's wing
Through violet eves—a poet born to sing;
Meanwhile his mate sleeps on secure; no cost
He counts for her—no time, no labour lost:
O Spring, so generous, so unreckoning!

Summer has bloom, and Autumn fruit, and skies,
Tear-dried by fragrant airs and hot noons'
breath—
But careless hang the nests, the birds far flown,
And leaf and grass bear sign of coming death.
Oh, for a Spring that changes not nor dies!
Oh, for a day like days that I have known!

II.

So April left me laughing 'neath the moon,
And turned her young face backwards sweet and
dear.
So May slipped by, and June rose-crowned was
here:
I could not weep for Spring—who weeps in June?

I was not tired as yet—who tires at noon?
  My buds were blown, my wheat was in the ear,
  My linnets sang—I dreamed not Death was near,
That Hope should die, that Joy should die so soon.

O friends, be patient if I weep to-day—
  To-day, to-morrow, and for evermore—
  Forsake me not, stay by my lonely door,
And sometimes lift the latch if you but say:
  She weeps such tears as broken hearts have
    shed—
  She weeps so long, 'twere better she were dead!

THE SPRING BIRDS.

THE glad spring birds are singing, singing;
   See them, hear them, far and near,
Sweetly on the still air flinging
   Bursts of music low and clear;
Skylark, blackbird, ·linnet grey,
Swallow, thrush, and goldfinch gay.
List, their voices float along—
While a soul seems in each song—
Through bright meadows, where the flowers
Crimson blush 'mid summer hours,
By the lake that pensive lies
Dreaming 'neath the quiet skies,—
Over rivers in full glee
Rushing onward to the sea,—
Lost in gossamer cloudlets white,
Half a shadow, half sunbeam bright,—
High and low in the trembling air,
Hear their voices everywhere.
And groweth your heart not young to-day,
With the joyous song-birds on the way?
With a tender dream of the love and truth,
The unquestioning trust of your far-off youth,
When careless and free as the bird's wild strain
The young glad life had no thought of pain.

But hark ! those low notes, streaming, streaming—
   Three full words with mournful air ;
Upon yon chestnut, blossom-beaming,
   Mark you not the robin there ?
Has his voice for you no sound
More than birds that sing around ?—
Does it bear no mystic spell,
And no tale of far years tell—
While the dead and parted throng
Who with you once heard his song ?
Do you think of weed-grown graves—
And the parting, moaning waves—
And the farewell on the shore,
And the voice you'll hear no more ?
Does he call back childhood's playing
And the young heart's fervent praying ?
Or speaks his strain of dark to-morrow
Of tears and pain and lonely sorrow,
Of the listless hands and the friendless years,
Of the snows of age and its unknown fears ?
Ah ! sad and strange to my heart to-day,
Comes many a dream from the far away,
As the robin's song has stirred this hour
Memory's chords with their tender power.

TWILIGHT.

THE swallows pass before my sight,
  And plunge so low in circling bands,
  That children stretch out eager hands
And think to catch them in their flight.

At last, at last, the day is done—
  The fiery shafts pale in the west,
  And man and earth are glad to rest,
Half sorrowful from toil and sun.

I hear the children still at play
  Among the graves up in the yard—
  Ah ! yet more thoughtless and more hard
We pass by sadder things each day.

Far on the moor some wild bird screams—
  The strange, wild voice of homeless things—
  A tired crane sails on listless wings
To her lone rest by silent streams.

The air is heavy still with heat,
  Deep stars break through the purple sky,
  Soft clouds unite the hill-tops high,
Like parted souls in dreams that meet.

On that low branch of lilac near
   One robin sings his song alone :
   Ah ! tell me, singer, hast thou known
The last fond look of things most dear ?

And outside in the silent street,
   So soiled with sin, and wrong, and strife,
   Some wearied woman weaves her life
Into pathetic music sweet.

I dream a hand rests on my head,
   Ah ! laid in dust these eight long years —
   Poor hand I moistened once with tears,
Come back in blessing from the dead !

And linger yet, you loved me best—
   The deep, still air with fragrance thrills,
   The blue waves clasp the flower-girt hills—
For just this hour I'd break your rest.

I know not how, or whence, or why,
   My heart is full this summer light,
   And Life says solemn things to-night,
And strange dreams pass me slowly by.

My absent friend ! you have done well,
   Your strong heart has subdued its strength,
   And to the Cross for breadth and length,
The proud will chained with magic spell.

Your lips are sweet from constant prayer,
   Your hands are browned from good deeds
     wrought,
   Your sad, dark eyes speak tender thought,
And all your face breathes mountain air.

So far from all that once was dear,
   In foreign home and foreign grave,
   Yet there the verdant grass will wave,
The wild-flowers grow as sweet as here.

Oh, stay! your heart is large and glad,
   More true and kind each changing year,
   The summer air is soft and clear,
And all my soul to-night is sad.

BESIDE THE SUIR.

BEYOND where the branching trees divide,
  In the tender light of the dying day,
See the Suir's gold track where the waters glide
  Towards the crumbling arch in a shower of spray :
Away o'er the rocks like a frightened thing,
  With a rush and roar through the narrow space,
Then out with a happy murmuring,
  A laugh, and a ripple, and dimpled face.

There's the convent grey and the spire above,
  With its clear back-ground of the deep blue
    skies,
I can see every spot in that place I love,
  As I stand here now and I close my eyes :
And 'twas never half in the past so dear,
  Nor drew my thoughts with such love away,
Not one half as fair as I see it here,
  A picture framed in my heart to-day.

I know every stone in those ivied walls,
  From the shaded walk to the terrace high ,
I know where the green of the spring first falls
  And the roses latest in summer die ;

Where the strong floods swirl in the autumn days
   When the waters rush with a troubled speech
From the wind-swept hills, where the lightning plays,
   From the bare brown bog, where the wild geese
      screech.

On the Suir's green margin the sweet flowers grow
   And they seem not to me so sweet elsewhere,
And the waters linger as loath to go,
   Through the blossomed reeds and the rushes
      there,
The forget-me-not and the woodruff tall,
   The strawberry blossoms that grow in the dells,
And the fairest flower still of them all—
   The frail and trembling white sorrel-bells :

The fair, white bells on the banks that lie
   On their thick-strewn leaves of the tenderest
      green,
On that soft pavilion laid out to die,
   With the purple streaks in their pallid sheen,
Too pure and fair on the earth to stay,
   In no common mould must they find a grave,
They'll droop and pine on their thrones away
   Ere the parching sun shines full on the wave.

And the river whispers as past it flies
   Of the tears that fall in a tempest rain,
From the sleepless grief of a mourner's eyes
   Whilst " God's will be done," saith she in her
      pain :

And it whispers, too, that a heart is weighed,
  Is weighed and measured as weight of gold,
And the wealth of the love and the memories laid
  In its depths, by the strength of its pain is told.

Thank God, but once in this dread eclipse,
  Can death come darkening window and door,
Till "my sun is set," say the trembling lips,
  "My day is done," saith the heart all sore :
The light is gone from the golden paths,
  Rise the moon and stars in a tenderer sway,
The pale flowers droop for their evening baths,
  And seaward the river rushes away.

THE POOR.

THEIR lot is hard, their pleasures few,
    Their lives one page of toil ;
From morning's dawn to evening's dew,
    Still tired hands till rough soil.
With want and pain and care untold,
    Their daily path is spread ;
Through sun and heat, through frost and cold,
    The poor must work for bread.

Then let your ways be kind and sweet,
    Considerate evermore—
For ah ! God knows, enough they meet
    To make a strong heart sore.
Be gentle in each word and deed,
    Attentive while they speak,
And give them help in their sore need
    When old and sick and weak.

There are who can no want make known—
    Proud natures, strange and shy,
Who'd bear e'en hunger, and alone
    Endure until they die ;
Seek such as these with timely aid,
    Seek them with gentle grace,
Remembering you will be repaid
    Where mercy holds first place.

A swaying leaf will crush a flower,
    A deed unkind the heart,
And wounds are made in one short hour,
    That through a life may smart.
The thoughtless word can give deep pain,
    And open scars unseen :
For feelings quick the poor retain,
    None feel a slight more keen.

Young children, too, that toil all day,
    With small hands hard and brown,
Who should be in the fields at play,
    Where merry feet run down.
With faces pinched from want and woe,
    Sad, prematurely old—
Alas ! alas ! it must be so,
    For bread their youth is sold.

Ah ! pity them so young and weak,
    So fragile and so small ;
Be tender in your ways and seek
    Their soul's good over all.
The Saviour keeps each kindness shown
    Safe in His Heart, be sure,
To these His little ones, His own,
    The children of His poor.

No need to seek Him far away,
    He dwells where they remain,
With humble souls He loves to stay
    'Mid sickness, want, and pain.

The poor, the friendless, the despised—
  The outcast and the low :
Make these your friends, nor be surprised
  If blessings round you flow.

God bless the poor man and his home,
  His little ones, his all ;
God guard each path where he may roam
  At labour's ceaseless call :
His summers short, his winters long,
  His life's hard daily part,
God bless his tears, and bless his song,
  God bless his patient heart.

A FAVOURITE NOOK.

'TIS little changed—the old, dear spot,
   The willows bending softly o'er,
The noisy stream, the shaded pond,
   The river murmuring as before.

I know the robin sings each eve,
   Thy favourite strain on yonder tree,
The few rich notes so clear and sweet,
   So sadly twined with thoughts of thee.

The tired crane stoops from wearied flight,
   To pause awhile in quiet here,
The dove complains, the restless wren
   Sings his sweet song in brambles near.

The whitethorn seat, girt round with moss,
   Where hyacinth pale and sorrel wave,
And wild pink sweet and drooping fern,
   Ah, me !—to-day I saw thy grave.

Two years ago we both stood here :—
   'Tis scarcely changed—the old, wild spot—
Two years ago, two swift long years,
   How soon the dead are heeded not !

A lock of hair all streaked with gray,
    A hundred tender thoughts of thee,—
Where thou art gone, pain has no part,
    And these are all now left to me.

Had I the power, no hand should touch
    A single branch once trained by thine ;
This place should ever sacred be
    To thy dear name, to auld-lang-syne.

But change must steal with time o'er all,
    And years must bring their changes here,
To tree, and flower, and shaded pond,
    To those few hearts who hold thee dear.

Always for me with grief comes back
    From our old days a night in May :
The robin sang, and paused and sang,
    And kept us listening to his lay.

And as I stand where long that night
    We stood while stars in glory shone,
Alone and sad this hour I know,
    The best friend of my life is gone.

The oldest friend, the longest tried,
    The dearest, kindest, best to me !
Through time, through tears, I realize
    How much Death took from Life with thee.

Around this favourite haunt of thine,
   My lingering footsteps often range ;
Had I the power no human hand
   One single branch, one stone should change.

SAFE.

THE snow is deep and the winds cry loud,
   While the treacherous icebergs float at sea ;
The wolf looks up to the swaying shroud—
   And the ship may sail, but it bears not me.

The savage is fierce, and the desert lone,
   The jackal cries for his prey all night ;
The king may win or may lose a throne :
   I go not hence to join in the fight.

The world is fickle, and false are friends,—
   My heart is mine, and my fair broad lands,
Rash venture soon in disaster ends—
   I lock my heart and I close my hands.

The ship came home o'er the harbour-bar
   And the sailor-lad to his mother brought ;
The soldier crowned came back from the war ;
   While the heart was wrecked that would venture
     nought.

THE MONTH OF THE SACRED HEART.

Just now, and the varied shades of green
  Stood out 'gainst the soft May sky full clear ;
The lilac bloomed, and the chestnut waved,
  And the fragrant thorn hid blushing near.
All day came the corncrake's twisted note,
  The swallow's song with the stream made tune,
While the summer hours kept chiming sweet
  Their prelude low for the coming June.

For the deep mid-June and the Sacred Heart—
  The Heart transpierced and the crimson tide,
The lance and rays, and the open wound,
  Where the stricken ones and the bruised may
    hide.
Have our lips for Him no words of love ?
  Our souls no want, or no pain our life ?
Was there never a hope from our hearts that died
  Nor a fair dream crushed in the world's rude
    strife ?

As none beside, will He feel for us ;
  No pang or pain but His Heart once bore—
The parted friend and the fresh green grave ;
  The chill neglect and the spirit sore ;

The unkind word, and the thoughtless act,
  And the kindness done that met poor return—
He knows them all, and He is our God,
  Whose Heart with pity and love doth burn.

The wild bird cooleth his purple wing
  Where the lazy leaves still float alway,
The lily bends and the red rose droops,
  And rapture breathes o'er the earth to-day.
'Tis our Lord's own Feast, the Feast of Love—
  He pleads, as once by the olive tree,
From yearning depths of a human heart,
  "Could you not watch yet an hour with me?"

We'll watch and pray, and we'll come to Him,
  With the bleeding rose and the lily white,
The mignonette and the scented thyme,
  And trembling star of the jasmine slight.
We'll bring the flowers, and we'll bring our hearts
  Our wants shall plead, and our weakness pray,
For 'tis love's own feast, in deep mid-June,
  And God can reject no prayer to-day.

A KIND WORD.

WHERE the earth is rich in beauty
  'Mid the fair Egyptian clime
Went Macarius forth on duty
  With a brother at noontime.
And the fervid sun was burning,
  As he passed, on mercy bent,
To Christ's little ones, oft turning,
  And on holy things intent.

While his prayers thus softly telling,
  With a tender, gentle mien—
Seemed it that his mind was dwelling
  On some sad and far-off scene.
Never heeding that the brother
  Had gone quicker by the road ;
So his thoughts were on Another,
  Toiling 'neath the Cross's load.

Now he saw his Saviour falling—
  Wounded, bleeding to the ground—
Now he heard rough voices calling,
  As they strike Him gathered round.

Through his prayers his tears came faster—
    Ah ! he often shed those tears,
For the sweet and gentle Master
    He had served so many years.

Well he marked Christ's deep compassion,
    In that hour, for human woe—
For the toil, the pain, and passion,
    Which man suffers here below.
For the souls tried by temptation,
    Dear and precious to His Heart,
And whose fearful desolation
    He had chosen for His part.

Saw His pity for the weary,
    For the poor still first His own,
And whose pathway hard and dreary
    He had travelled and had known :
For the hands that toil for ever,
    For the lives in sorrow spent,
Tender hearts that death would sever,
    Kindred ties with heart's blood rent.

And the saint with great love burning
    Just a moment paused and prayed,
To his bleeding Master turning—
    All his soul with pity swayed ;
Asking more of tender feelings,
    Greater heart to feel for all,
For all pain in sad revealings,
    For all bitter tears that fall.

Hot the noonday sun and broiling,
  While there came along the road
A poor heathen priest, swift toiling—
  Panting 'neath a heavy load.
" May the sweet Lord give you blessing,
  He who for your ransom bled ; "
" You are kind in thus addressing,"
  Laying down the load, he said.

"Nay, poor man," and tender smiling
  Lit the gentle, pallid face,
" I but spoke that thus beguiling
  You might rest a little space."
Oh ! the holy power of kindness,
  That can move the human heart,
Oh ! the power that e'en to blindness
  Can a healing grace impart !

Just a short while since the brother
  Passed with aspect cold and stern,
No harsh word his lips could smother,
  Nothing mild or gracious learn,
Though Macarius chided often,
  And at prayer had made request,
That the Saviour meek would soften
  That hard heart as He knew best.

So the monk, with fervour fired,
  Passed the strange priest on the road,
Much distressed, and hot and tired,
  Bending 'neath a heavy load,

Rough his words of salutation,
  Till the heathen, angered more,
With a furious exclamation,
  Turned and left him bruised and sore.

St. Macarius had done kindly,
  And God's grace came swift and sweet
To the heathen's heart, and blindly,
  Humbly, knelt he at his feet :
Changed and gentle, earnest pleading
  The true God to serve and know,
And with eager interceding
  Begging with the saint to go.

ST. VINCENT'S LAST VISIT TO HIS FATHER'S HOUSE.

THE leaves shook softly in the wind,
The glad birds sang upon the hillsides grey,
When Vincent started for the distant way,
    Leaving his father's home behind

A heavy sadness marked his face,
Like Christ's the hour He stole from Mary's side
For three days' lengthening agony to hide,
    She, seeking still from place to place.

The dark pine-woods stretched far away,
For ever restless 'neath the peaceful skies
There seemed sad murmur of farewells to rise
    From everything he loved to-day.

He heard the sweet Adour below
Keep singing softly in its rocky bed,
And all the dark pines moaning overhead,
    As in his childhood long ago.

Pathetic pictures thrilled his soul :
The morning memories of a dearer day;
The sweetness of a music passed away
    Came back with grief beyond control.

He saw his mother, aged and pale,
Stand listening for the step to come no more;
He saw his father watch him from the door,
Along the violet-blossomed vale.

He felt the radiance gone from sight,
The sinless glory of the far-off past,
The lights God quencheth one by one so fast,
Submerging in a sweeter light.

He could not leave without complaint
The paths white feet of childhood tracked long since;
The breezes passing by bore fragrance hence,
Tender and delicate and faint.

Like streams that from high hills depart,
Made rich by dews, by sun, and fertile rain,
Flooding with wealth each waste and arid plain,
A something such was Vincent's heart.

A mine of gems, of love untold,
A tree with branches spreading broad and high,
Where birds built, and all weary things came nigh
For shelter from fierce heat or cold.

He heard the parched cicala's cry
The glad birds singing on the vine-clad slopes;
And still o'er all, the knell of earthly hopes,
Low buried, never more to rise.

He heard the babe's forsaken cry
Call to him from the cruel midnight street ;
The wail of millions, that with restless feet
    To sin and doom rushed madly by.

And hurrying forth with pallid face,
Far northwards to the distant, troubled Seine,
He never more, not ever once again
    Set foot within his native place.

A PASSAGE PAID.

'MID the forests grand and trackless,
  Far away within the West,
Where the settler built his log-hut,
  And the mocking bird her nest,
Lay a poor young Irish woodsman,
  Sick with fever and with pain,
All his brow was flushed to crimson,
  All his life-sweat poured like rain.

There was need of careful nursing,
  And the stranger was most kind,
Tending to the dry lips burning,
  To the restless, wandering mind;
He had hewn the mighty timbers,
  He had cleared the lonely glade,
For long months the echoes trembled
  To his axe's sounding blade.

All his work was for his dear ones—
  For the mother whose old days
Had been cheered with many comforts
  And relieved in many ways:
Though she'd feel, I know, more happy,
  And have made more thankful prayer,
Just to hear his glad laugh near her,
  To stroke down his dark-brown hair;

Just to catch his step at evening,
　　As he came before the door,
Or to mark him in his manhood,
　　Like his father years before :
When she died, they found a paper
　　Stained with tears, hid in a box—
One brown lock of hair, some letters,
　　And a child's small faded socks.

She was sleeping in Kilsheelan,
　　And last week a letter went,
Taking home two sisters' passage,
　　And a year's hard-earned rent ;
But another ship was sailing,
　　Guided by an angel's hand,
Sailing fast to bear him onwards,
　　To a fairer, better land.

Ah ! 'twas sad to hear him raving
　　Of the old familiar hills,
Where the music of his childhood
　　Sang in fifty murmuring rills;
Of his home in far Tipperary,
　　And the winding wild boreen,
Where the brown thrush sang the sweetest,
　　Where the leaves kept longest green ;

Of the football and the hurling,
　　Of the dance and of the fair ;
Talking of the pleasant places
　　And the kindly neighbours there ;

Driving home the cows for milking,
   And, as slow they browsing came,
In the dear old Irish language
   Chiding each with some pet name.

Ah ! 'twas sad to hear him telling,
   How the young shoots grew so fast,
Where last eve he leaped the hedgerow,
   Thorny, fragrant, like his past :
How he waded through the brown bog,
   Where the panting hare sought rest,
And green heath and sedge were shading
   Wild duck's eggs in sheltered nest.

Now the plough sank in the fallow,
   Stiff with weeds and damp and brown,
And he softly urged the horses,
   As they toiled the long field down ;
Ah ! 'twas sad to see him trying,
   The poor fellow in his pain,
To rise up and stroke the forehead,
   To smooth back the tangled mane.

They were simple things he clung to,
   And his life was much the same,
Yet I think God loved to see him
   When the summons later came.
'Twas an hour before the dawning,
   As his white lips moved in prayer,
That the angels softly called him,
   To that land where all is fair.

And I question, though I know not,
  When those angels call the roll,
'Mid the martyrs bearing branches
  Shall we see this poor boy's soul ?
I am sure his hands were spotless,
  All his heart was clean and true,
And he gave his life for others ;
  Not much more might martyr do.

HIS MOTHER.

OH ! there are hours when love will speak,
When memories crowd, and feelings throng
And words rush upward to the lips,
And shape themselves in tones of song.

As streams o'erflow in time of rain,
And music make along the way,
So kneeling here at Mary's feet,
My heart o'erflows with love to-day.

O gentle Lady ! gracious Queen !
O Lady ! good and kind to me,
I'd give my blood, I'd give my life,
To gain one glory more for thee !

Ah me ! what foolish words I speak—
Thou couldst not be more sweet and fair.
I have so many daily faults,
That wants alone must make my prayer.

O gentle Lady, gracious Queen !
Forgive a sinner's lay like mine,
When saintly hands write well thy praise,
And poet-hearts throb in each line.

And so 'twill be for evermore,
As swift the ages roll along ;
Love's pulse will thrill the burning rhyme,
While flows for thee the tide of song.

God wills it, and it must be so,
The lesson sweet Himself first taught—
He lisped thy name, He sought thy care,
To thee His childish sorrows brought.

He hid His face oft in thy robes,
And played with thee as children play ;
He marked thy smile, He caught thy sigh,
He thought of thee by night and day.

He watched within the quiet house,
While thou wouldst take the needed rest ;
He made the fire, He fetched the wood,
He listened for thy least behest.

He brought fresh water from the brook,
Where sang for Him bright gold-winged birds.
" 'Twill please my Mother," His fond thought,
" My Mother bids me," His sweet words.

Thy lightest wish was law to Him,
Thy slightest want His daily care ;
He prayed for sinners, prayed for me—
For thee His Mother, what His prayer !

He knelt to seek in manhood's prime
Thy blessing and thy leave that day,
Ere yet He went to give for us
The life He owed to thee away.

And so 'twill be through endless years,
As swift the ages roll along—
Love's pulse will thrill the burning rhyme,
And wake for thee the tide of song.

A DARK DAY.

STRONG men are preparing a home dark and lone,
 They're working in silence and sorrow—
Making a bed for a tired tender head,
A strange hard bed hewed from common gray
  stone,
 Where he will be sleeping to-morrow :
And bells are ringing, and sweet psalms singing,
And tears to a thousand eyes are springing.

They're building it narrow and straight and deep,
    Ah ! so deep and lonesome and dreary,
When not pillow of gold, nor soft white lily's fold,
Were fit for the place where he will sleep—
    Sleep sound from the hard road weary ;
When winds are sighing, and late flowers dying,
And all things sweet by a grave are lying.

Not fit were the soft, rich silken bands,
    Nor couch with rare jewels blazing ;
Not the diamond's breast for his heart were fit rest,
And the strong men work with white trembling hands,
    With eyes that are tear-dimmed gazing ;
While winds are wailing and roses failing,
And each sweet dead hope in a coffin's nailing.

They dig deep down, they hammer and bore,
    Such a strange, sharp sound ever making
Do they think all the day as they're toiling away
That they dig most sure to one bruised heart's core,
    One heart with the dread pain breaking ?
While flowers are falling, and sad winds calling,
And the thrilied air filled with a grief appalling.

Yet the sun is lighting for joy outside,
    The river gone mad with singing ;
Had I life for the tears of the centuries' years,
All joy in my heart from to-day had died,
    Died out at that dread sound ringing—
Poor heart sore aching ! poor heart surebreaking !
Poor heart that the storm's so soon o'ertaking !

October 30th, 1885.

PERHAPS there is an hour in other hours
  When I shall stand with bated breath, as now,
  And see another calm upon thy brow,
And watch a deeper sleep with heart-wrung showers.
And I should meet the daylight and the flowers,
  And words and smiles that happy hearts endow,
  Thou laid amongst the dead.   I yet should bow
And bare my trembling soul to Heaven's dread
    powers,
And face my life, and say, *Thy will be done.*
  I would not shirk a grief at cost to thee—
To save thee pain no earthly sorrow shun ;
  But oh ! I pray that hour may pass from me,
For thou art strong and nobler far to bear—
I pray my death that awful hour may spare.

A LONG FAREWELL.

THE hour I dreaded years ago has come
    And gone, and taken all things dear from me;
    The prayer I prayed that sweet June day, when
      bee
And flower and grass were sad with drowsy hum,
Has fallen unheard. Now desolate and dumb
    With pain, I lift two trembling hands to Thee,
    My God, and moan, " Thy will be done." Ah,
      me !
How sorrow makes the heart feel sick and numb !

Thou, far more dear than sky, or moon, or star,
    Or summer seas that rise in softest swell,
(And they were dear, and so was that June sun),
    Thou more to me than friends or life—farewell !
Farewell, till these few weary sands be run,
Farewell, till thy hand beckon from afar.

II.

My soul is jealous at the sight and sound
    And stir of busy, surging human life ;
    Strong hand, and earnest brain, and restless
      strife,
And full, free health, 'mid freshest airs abound.

The reapers laugh and sing in cornfields round,
   The deep, green woods with living things are rife,
   Whilst I—my heart as sore as though a knife
Had slit it wide—I sit upon the ground,

And hear, throughout the long, hot summer days,
   The tones of one sweet voice, drowning the fret
Of sounds discordant and perplexing ways ;
   With changeless, ineffectual regret,
I ever look upon one sad white face,
And all the happy past with tears retrace.

The Freeman's Journal, Limited, Printers, Dublin.

www.ingramcontent.com/pod-product-compliance
Lightning Source LLC
Chambersburg PA
CBHW030610270326
41927CB00007B/1108